ALL YOU NEED TO KNOW

Dinosaurs

68

Contents

First published in Great Britain by
Cherrytree Books, part of the Evans Publishing Group
2A Portman Mansions
Chiltern Street
London W1U 6NR

Copyright © this edition Evans Brothers Limited 2004

Originally published under the title
'Mes Petites Encyclopédies Larousse Les dinosaures'
Copyright © LAROUSSE/VUEF 2002
Copyright © LAROUSSE/S.E.J.E.R 2004

Text by Agnès Vandewiele, Michèle Lancina

ISBN 1 84234 233 9

A CIP catalogue record for this book is available from the British Library

Printed in France

ALL YOU NEED TO KNOW ABOUT...

Dinosaurs

Illustrated by **Clotilde Perrin**

CHERRYTREE BOOKS

Before the dinosaurs

Before dinosaurs appeared on Earth about 230 million years ago, there were already reptiles like the dimetrodon.

There were
giant dragonflies…

…and amphibians,
like the ichtyostega.

All sorts of dinosaurs

We already know of more than a thousand different species of dinosaurs. And every year more new dinosaur skeletons are found. Here are just some of the different kinds of dinosaurs.

Seismosaurus was an enormous dinosaur, as long as five buses.

Compsognathus was one of the smallest dinosaurs, at about a metre long.

Brachiosaurus was one of the largest and heaviest dinosaurs. It could weigh up to 80 tons!

Styracosaurus had a spiky ruff around its neck, a horn on its nose and a beak.

The most famous

Stegosaurus was larger than an elephant. But its brain was no bigger than a nut!

Triceratops, with its three horns, looked a bit like a rhinoceros. It charged at its enemies to defend itself.

Euoplocephalus was covered in thick plates of armour and had a tail shaped like a club.

Corythosaurus had a crest on the top of its head. The crest helped it to attract a mate.

Velociraptor was about as big as
a goat and could run very fast.
And beware of its terrible claws!

Diplodocus was a gentle giant with
a small head and an extremely
long neck. It only ate leaves.

Iguanadon was armed with
enormous spikes on its thumbs.

The terrible Tyrannosaurus,
most feared of all the dinosaurs,
had long, razor-sharp teeth.

The age of dinosaurs

The dinosaurs lived on Earth for about 165 million years.

Eoraptor was one of the first dinosaurs to appear on Earth about 228 million years ago. It was about the same size as a dog.

As the first forests appeared on the Earth, herbivorous (plant-eating) dinosaurs like Barosaurus and Brachiosaurus evolved.

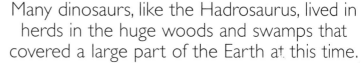

Many dinosaurs, like the Hadrosaurus, lived in herds in the huge woods and swamps that covered a large part of the Earth at this time.

What were the dinosaurs?

The word 'dinosaur' means 'terrifying lizard'. Like today's lizards, the dinosaurs were reptiles. Their skin was covered in scales and they laid eggs.

But unlike other reptiles, such as crocodiles and snakes, the dinosaurs didn't crawl or slither. They walked on two or four legs.

The **plant-eaters**

Sauropods had very long necks
that helped them reach the leaves
at the top of tall conifer trees.

Hadrosauruses had big, flat teeth,
which meant they could eat
even the toughest plants.

Many dinosaurs were herbivorous, which means that they ate plants, leaves, roots and seeds – but no grass, because it didn't exist at the time!

The Stegosaurus loved to eat ferns and mosses.

Carnivores and herbivores

Carnivorous (meat-eating) dinosaurs could run very fast to catch their prey.

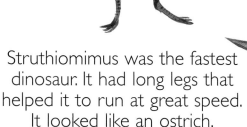

Gallimimus had a sharp, toothless beak. It mainly ate lizards and eggs.

Struthiomimus was the fastest dinosaur. It had long legs that helped it to run at great speed. It looked like an ostrich.

The deadly Deinonychus had a big hooked claw on each foot.

Dromiceiomimus could run at speeds of up to 50 km/h.

Herbivorous dinosaurs often moved
around in groups to protect themselves
from the carnivorous dinosaurs.

The **long-necked giants**

The long-necked dinosaurs (sauropods)
were the largest animals ever to have lived on Earth.

Mamenchisaurus had the longest neck of all time. It could stretch as high up as the third floor of a building.

Brachiosaurus looked like a giant giraffe.

Diplodocus's neck helped it to reach deep into thick forests to find food.

Strange heads

Some dinosaurs had weird and wonderful heads.

Torosaurus was very striking, with an enormous three-horned head and a huge ruff.

Corythosaurus had a fan-shaped, hollow crest on its head. Males had larger crests than females.

Tsintaosaurus had a horn between its eyes and a beak or bill, like a duck.

Parasaurolophus had a long crest on its head. The end of the crest could slot into a notch on its back.

Carnotaurus had two horns above its eyes.

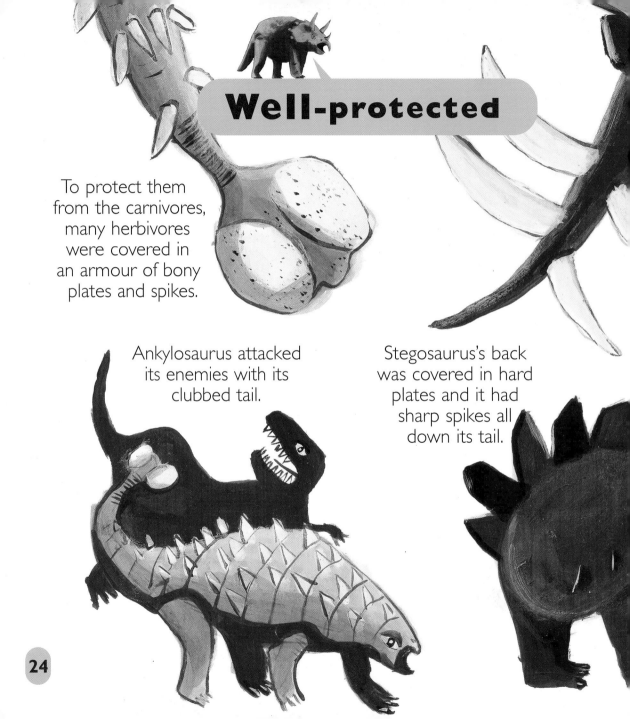

Well-protected

To protect them from the carnivores, many herbivores were covered in an armour of bony plates and spikes.

Ankylosaurus attacked its enemies with its clubbed tail.

Stegosaurus's back was covered in hard plates and it had sharp spikes all down its tail.

Torosaurus could defend itself with its three horns. Its huge ruff also helped to make it look frightening.

The **hunter** dinosaurs

Carnivorous (meat eating) dinosaurs ate herbivorous dinosaurs, as well as other animals.

Velociraptors often hunted in packs.

Deinonychus tore its prey apart with its enormous, sharp claws.

The terrible Tyrannosaurus hunted alone. It could eat up to 230 kg of meat and bones in just one bite.

At the time of the dinosaurs

The dinosaurs weren't alone on Earth. Many other creatures existed at the same time. Here are some of them.

flies

dragonflies

frogs and turtles

butterflies

flying reptiles
called pterosaurs

lizards

crocodiles

snakes

29

In the sky

The first creatures
to fly weren't birds.
They were reptiles,
cousins of the dinosaurs.

The first feathered bird
was the Archaeopteryx.
It had a long tail and teeth.
It flew very badly!

30

Quetzalcoatlus was the biggest flying creature of all time, with a wingspan of about 10 metres. It didn't have feathers. Instead it had leathery wings, a bit like a bat.

In the sea

There were fish, amphibians
and reptiles in the seas,
but these creatures weren't dinosaurs.

Ichthyosauruses looked like dolphins.
They had sleek, streamlined bodies
and were fast swimmers.

Elasmosaurus had a very
long neck and four
flippers. It ate fish and
other swimming creatures.

Why did they **disappear?**

The dinosaurs mysteriously vanished from Earth about 65 million years ago. Researchers have found many possible explanations for their disappearance.

A huge rock called a meteorite could have crashed into Earth from space. The impact would have killed many dinosaurs and other animals.

An ice age could have frozen the Earth for many years.

There could also have been huge volcanic eruptions which changed the Earth's climate and made it impossible for the dinosaurs to survive.

35

Records

Brachiosaurus: as tall as
a four-storey building.

The **longest**

Seismosaurus: as long as an
Olympic-sized swimming pool.

The longest **neck**

Mamenchisaurus: the creature
with the longest-ever neck,
up to around 15 metres.

The smallest

Compsognathus: about a metre long, the same size as a large chicken.

The biggest **head**

Pentaceratops: a head up to 3 metres long, the length of a small car.

The biggest **brain**

Troodon: the biggest brain in relation to its size. It was about as intelligent as a modern-day bird.

The **fastest**

Struthiomimus: could run as fast as a scooter.

Index